George

Patron of England

by
J.B. Midgley

*All booklets are published thanks to the
generous support of the members of the
Catholic Truth Society*

CATHOLIC TRUTH SOCIETY
PUBLISHERS TO THE HOLY SEE

Contents

Acknowledgements

The Catholic Truth Society gratefully acknowledges recourse to the following sources: *Catholic Dictionary*, Virtue and Co. Ltd, London, 1951. *Catholic Encyclopaedia*, The Encyclopaedia Press, London, 1907. *Catechism of the Catholic Church*, Geoffrey Chapman, London, 1993. *The Jerusalem Bible*, Darton, Longman & Todd, London, 1974. *The Divine Office*, Collins, London, 1974. *Catholic Commentary on the Holy Scripture*, Thomas Nelson & Sons, London 1951. *Papal Documents*, Catholic Truth Society, London. *History of Christianity*, Owen Chadwick, Weidenfeld and Nicolson, London 1995. *Eusebius of Caesarea* (translations), G.A.Williamson, Harmondsworth, London 1965. *The Westminster Hymnal*, Burns, Oates & Washbourne, London 1948. *Hymns Ancient and Modern*, William Clowes & Sons, London 1938. *Songs of Praise*, Oxford University Press, London 1931. *The Lives of the Fathers and Martyrs*, Father Alban Butler, Virtue & Co. Ltd, London.

England's Patron

When a nation is beset by divisions within itself, the message of Our Lord's Death and Resurrection is that reconciliation, forgiveness, sympathy, and encouragement are the means that resolve conflict and suspicion. When countries and societies are increasingly and misguidedly described as post-Christian, it is sensible to turn again to England's Patron for his caring intercession for the population and help for the Sovereign, Government and legitimate authority.

Desiderius Erasmus, the great Catholic humanist and friend of Saint Thomas More, offers a salutary and energizing reflection in his tribute: "O splendid England, home and citadel of virtue and learning. No land in all the world is like England. In no country would I love better to spend my days."

'Lord, you have given us cause to rejoice in the merits and intercession of your blessed martyr George. Grant that we who seek your favours through him may obtain them as a gift of your grace' (*Collect of the Liturgy of the Feast*).

Downham Market, Feast of Saint George,
23 April 2007

Why Patron Saints?

Christians honour holy men and women and acknowledge their virtuous lives that illuminate the path to God through His Son, Jesus Christ. The Blessed Virgin Mary and the Saints are holy because their lives conform to that of Our Lord, manifest the inherent values of the Gospel, and give a model for the Christian life. In the days when the Church was persecuted, special homage was paid to the martyrs who suffered to the point of death, and their cult united Christians in a common memory and devotional practice that invoked their intercession. When the age of persecution came to an end with the Peace of Constantine in 313 AD, the cult of martyrs extended beyond the "red", martyrdom of shedding blood to "white" martyrdom that included those who severed themselves from the mainstream of worldly life as ascetics and monks in lonely places, who suffered imprisonment or ill-usage for their Faith, or fulfilled the obligations of life, that has been described as "the fearsome daily round," with heroic and persevering fortitude.

Patron Saints

There have been moments in the history of the Church when the relationship between the Saints and Our Lord has led to the misconception that Saints were being worshipped. The teaching of the Church maintains the important distinction that only God is worshipped, while Mary and the Saints are appropriately honoured in private and public devotions that enrich the worship of God through Christ in the Holy Spirit. Individual people, occupation groups, dioceses, and countries venerate particular Saints as their special protectors, guardians, and intercessors who are called upon to help find solutions to a variety of problems. A person's patron saint is usually the one whose name is received at Baptism, or when the religious life is embraced. So, in the United States for example, the patron Saint is the Blessed Virgin Mary in her title of the Immaculate Conception, and Saint George watches over England where 82% of the population of Great Britain live. In a special way, patron saints intercede with Our Lord for the forgiveness of offences, give help in those times of temptation when the Devil makes assaults on souls, encourage good deeds, and offer comfort in misfortunes and distress.

Saints usually become patrons of countries, professions, and special needs through popular devotion and custom rather than by any official designation and appointment.

They may have been associated with the history of a country, or engaged in the work of a profession, or have exercised a ministry or healing related to a recognized need. It is admitted that sometimes the connection is difficult to identify, but the Holy Spirit ensures that the devotion is made holy and valid, and that the Saints in the Church Triumphant always respond to the prayers the faithful direct heavenwards. Even though some names no longer appear in the Roman Calendar, travellers need not think that their confidence in Saint Christopher is misplaced.

Patriotism and Nationhood

The Fathers of the Second Vatican Council, 1962-65, reminded Christians that as citizens they should develop a loyal devotion to their country while remaining concerned for "the welfare of the entire human family that is united by the bonds that link races, peoples, and nations." They said that, "Christians gathered together in the Church of all nations, live for God and Christ by following the honourable customs of their own nation. As other good citizens, they practise true and effective patriotism, and foster a universal love for humanity without racial prejudice or bitter nationalism" (cf. *'Pastoral Constitution on the Church in the Modern World'* 75, and *'Decree on the Missionary Activity of the Church'*, Article 3: 'Forming the Christian Community').

Towards the end of his life, Pope John Paul II pointed out that the responsibility of Patriotism (from the Latin *'pater'*, 'father') is included in the Fourth Commandment to honour one's father and mother who represent God the Creator in giving us life. Through them is acquired the spiritual patrimony of one's native land that provides the reason for the duty of 'pietas', the religious dimension of the veneration to which they are entitled. Patriotism is a love for everything that is to do with that land: its history, traditions, language and natural features, and it extends to the work of our compatriots and their achievements. It understands that the common good of all citizens requires accepting a responsibility to serve the continuing evolvement of social structure. It recognizes that, even in an age of supranational structures and internationalism, the native land, like the family, remains a permanent reality, and that the 'natural' societies of family and nation, far from being mere conventions, are part of human nature's social dimension. A society's cultural and historical identity is preserved within the concept of nation (Latin *'natus'*, 'born'), but its function must not degenerate into nationalism that involves pursuing the good of one's nation alone. Patriotism is a love of one's native land that accords to other nations the rights claimed for one's own, and leads to a properly ordered social love (cf. John Paul II, *'Memory and Identity'*, 2005).

In the context of Saint George's patronage, the belligerent tendencies of fallen humanity and the vocabulary come to mind, with an opportunity to reflect on what the Church says about warfare. In his letter of 1917 to the nations involved in the First World War, Pope Benedict XV pointed out that to prevent war and achieve permanent peace, material force must be replaced by moral right, there should be international agreement for the reduction of armaments, and a process of arbitration be applied to all international disputes. Exaggerated nationalism and militarist assumptions that wars are inevitable are obstacles to peace in the world. In his *Peace Letter to the World*, Christmas 1922, Pope Pius XI added that to prevent the moral and material destruction of civilization, and ensure the peace of the world, "the love of peace must be deeply rooted in our hearts. The Peace of Christ is the Reign of Christ."

Nearly half a century later, the Second Vatican Council re-affirmed relevant teaching in *'The Pastoral Constitution on the Church in the World of Today (Gaudium et Spes)'* If a nation or group of nations contemplates declaring war as a defence against aggression, the decision taken by those responsible for the common good must be subject to the evaluation of rigorous conditions of moral legitimacy. The damage inflicted by the aggressor must be certain, lasting, and grave; all other means of resolution should have been attempted and proved to be impractical and ineffective; there should be reasonable prospect of success; the use of arms must not cause more disorder than the evil that it is intended to eliminate and, in evaluating this condition, the power of modern means of destruction must be carefully considered. The Church and human reason assert the unchanging validity of the moral law during armed conflict, and the fact that war may have broken out does not mean that illegal behaviour on the part of the warring parties can ever be condoned. However, those who serve in the armed forces and carry out their duties honourably contribute to the common good of the nations and to the maintenance of peace (cf. *'Gaudium et Spes'* 78:5-80:3).

The Life of Saint George

According to an account given by the writer Metaphrastes, George was born about 275 AD to noble, Christian parents in Cappadocia, a Roman province in central Asia mentioned by Saint Peter at the beginning of his First Letter, about 275 AD. Some say that his father gave his life for the faith, and this may explain why his mother quickly took her young son to her homeland of Palestine where she owned a small estate that he eventually inherited. The boy grew into a fine man and became a soldier in the Roman army. His distinguished service soon earned the rank of tribune, comparable to colonel, and his courageous conduct brought further promotion from the emperor Diocletian himself.

In a barbaric age, Christianity shone in the world as the one power that could save it. It had acquired the strength of the Roman character, the best of Greek culture and, most of all, it was founded on Our Lord's incomparable moral teaching that attracted men and women who anxiously witnessed the disintegration of Rome. Unfortunately, Diocletian looked on this religion as a threat to imperial strength and influence, and considered it fit only for slaves and outcasts. He set about the task of destroying it, but his campaign only hastened the empire's demise.

Persecution

It was some time in 303 AD that the emperor began to persecute the Christians. George immediately resigned his commission, laid aside his own dignity, refused to deny his Faith, and made personal representation to Diocletian. He took him to task for his barbarous cruelty, and for this he was thrown into prison and subjected to cruel tortures that included being forced to run in red-hot sandals, having his body broken on a spiked wheel, being immersed in quicklime, and bound on the ground while a huge boulder was rolled on top of him. Nothing could shake his constancy however, and the following day he was led through the city of Lydda in Palestine, sometimes called Diospolis, and there beheaded.

Saint George is listed in the *Martyrology of Saint Jerome*, 341-420 and, in his decree of 495, Pope Saint Gelasius includes him among "those saints whose names are justly remembered amongst men but whose actions are known only to God." In assessing Saint George's status, it is significant that Pope Saint Gregory the Great, 590-604, restored a church dedicated to him in Rome, and included his name and cult in the Gregorian Sacramentary. This is a collection of prayers, prefaces, and rubrics for a liturgy that was to be celebrated by popes at the Lateran Basilica in Rome. This highest ranking Church in Christendom and the Episcopal seat of the Pope as Bishop of Rome, was built early in the fourth century as the Church of the Saviour on land given by Constantine, re-dedicated to Saint John the Baptist in 905 by Pope Sergius III, and was the official papal residence until its move to Avignon at the beginning of the "Babylonian Captivity" in 1309.

The decree of Pope Gelasius also acknowledges the existence of the *'Acts of Saint George'*, the earliest known narrative that recounts all the wonderful deeds he is said to have accomplished. Their marvellous character can be explained only by the enthusiasm of the oral tradition that adjusts and adds admiring details over time to improve a good story that had, nevertheless, some foundation of truth. In one episode, the Saint is put to death three times, first by being chopped into little pieces, and then buried deep in the earth, and finally consumed by fire, but on each occasion he is resuscitated by the power of God. There are stories of the dead being restored to life so as to be baptized, wholesale conversions to the Faith, instantaneous destruction of armies and idols, beams of wood bursting into leaf, and milk flowing from the martyr's severed head instead of blood.

Legend or real?

Nothing described as legendary necessarily weakens the forceful historical argument of Saint George's existence that is made by the devotion that sprang up in specific localities almost immediately after his death. Lactantius in his *'Death of the Persecutors'*, and his contemporary Eusebius, the Father of Church History, 260-339, both identify the courageous soldier who tore down Diocletian's edict of persecution at Nicomedia, and consequently gave his life for the Faith. A church was soon dedicated to Saint George the Martyr in Thessalonika, and discovered inscriptions point to the fact that there were others in Syria, Mesopotamia and Egypt, all before the end of the fourth century. The *Martyrology* of Saint Bede the Venerable, 673-735, reveals that he has been known in England since the seventh century, and he is also included in the *Irish Martyrology* of Saint Oengus who died in 824. Aelfric, also known as Grammaticus, a prominent figure in Anglo-Saxon literature and the great prose writer of his time, includes the story of the fight with the Dragon in his *'Lives of the Saints'*, 996.

Devotion to Saint George

Christendom's extraordinary devotion and recourse to
Saint George is an indication of the Church's appreciation
of his name and triumphs, and she honours him as one of
her most illustrious martyrs for the Faith. The Eastern
Church soon included him in the list of the greatest
martyrs, and the Greeks distinguished him by the title of
"The Great Martyr". Within a few years, the emperor
Constantine, 258-357, had built six churches in
Constantinople and dedicated them to his honour and,
according to the author of the 'Gesta Francorum', he also
built the church of Saint George that stands over the
martyr's tomb at Ramleh in Palestine.

Long before the end of the fourth century, Byzantine
armies were entrusting their exploits and campaigns to
Saint George's special care, and their historians were
recording the many battles that were won, and the
miraculous events that took place through his
intercession. During the fifth and sixth centuries growing
numbers of pilgrims made their way to the Holy Land to
visit the places sanctified by Our Lord and walk in His
footsteps. They were moved by the stories about Saint
George's valour and edifying death, visited his churches

and tomb, and having learned to venerate him, brought devotion to the West, particularly France. Saint Clotilde, 475-545, who was the wife of Clovis, the first Christian king of the Francs, erected many sanctuary altars to Saint George, and Clovis himself built a monastery in his name at Baralle about 512. The eminent hymn writer Venantius Fortunatus, 530-609, to whom we owe such treasures as *'Vexilla Regis'* (The royal banners forward go), *'Pange lingua gloriosi'* (Sing my tongue of warfare ended), *'Quem terra Pontus, sidera'* (The God whom earth, and sea, and sky), and *'O gloriosa virginum'* (Queen on whose starry brow doth rest), wrote epigrammatic verses in praise of Saint George for his church built in Mentz.

In the middle of the sixth century, the Byzantine emperor, Justinian I, commissioned a new church in the Saint's honour to be built at Bizanes in Lower Armenia, and the emperor Mauritius founded another magnificent edifice in Constantinople. According to his biographer, the historian Eleusius, the holy monk Saint Theodore of Sykeon, 540-613, who became bishop of Anastasiopolis, had an ardent devotion to Saint George, prayed frequently and fervently to him in a specially dedicated chapel, and encouraged the emperor Mauritius to follow his example and seek his intercession. By happy coincidence Saint Theodore's Feast is on April 22nd, the day before that of Saint George.

The Story of Saint George and the Dragon

The origin of the story is obscure but there are precedents of dragon slayers, or problem solvers, in early literature like the Christian Theodore of Heraeclaea, Agapetus, and Arsacius, all of whom were historical persons. There has been some conjecture that it is just an allegorization of Diocletian who is referred to as a dragon in the *'Legenda Aurea'* by Jacobus a Voragine, 1230-1298. This mediaeval manual of ecclesiastical tradition included lives of the saints with suggested homilies for their feasts, and a commentary on the liturgy. It was translated into English and printed by William Caxton about 1478 as *'The Golden Legend'*, and publication refreshed and widened Saint George's popularity. He is presented as the youngest and bravest champion of Christendom and the personification of chivalry. He is already referred to as Saint George, and obviously had been canonized by popular acclaim long before the formal process was introduced about the twelfth century. Since his cult had preceded the *'Legenda Aurea'* by at least eight centuries, the accusation that the Church had somehow "converted and baptized the pagan Greek hero Perseus" who had killed a sea monster at Lydda is unjustified.

A fearsome dragon had been ravaging the countryside around Selena, a pagan city in Libya, and had made its den in a marshy swamp where the waters were deep. Its foul breath caused pestilence as it roamed through the land, and whenever it threatened the city, the inhabitants gave it two sheep to satisfy its hunger. When the supply of sheep eventually became exhausted, the citizens adopted the desperate practice of offering a human victim who was selected by the drawing of lots. The King was devastated when the lot fell upon his youngest daughter, and he offered the people a huge sum of money to choose a substitute but they refused. The Princess Sabra insisted that she fulfil her duty and, dressed as a bride, set off bravely to her fate in the marshy swamp.

It happened that Saint George rode by on his trusty steed, clad in shining armour, and his marvellous sword Ascalon at his side. He saw the noble maiden walking towards the marsh, her beautiful face pale and fearful. The splendid Knight galloped towards her, but when she heard him coming she turned and cried, 'Flee young Knight, or you too will perish.' 'God forbid that I should flee when a maiden is in peril,' Saint George answered but, even as he spoke, the waters of the marsh in front of them rose in great waves with a roaring sound. The people, who were standing on the walls of the city that was built on high ground overlooking the marsh, began to wail and wring their hands.

The sound of the roaring grew louder, and the Princess cried, 'Flesh and blood cannot withstand the burning flame that comes from the monster's mouth. It has destroyed two armies of soldiers, eaten our sheep and cattle, and devastated my father's kingdom. Escape while you can and do not risk your life by trying to defend me.' As she spoke, the waters rose in great waves and the roaring grew louder and louder. Saint George scarcely had time to grasp his lance and raise his shield before the dragon was upon him. It was truly a terrible monster, and looked like an enormous serpent with four great wings and four huge feet armed with cruel claws, and its tailed was armed with a long, poisonous sting.

The dragon rushed upon Saint George, a burning flame issuing from its jaws and, with a flap of its great wing, felled him to the ground. As it came upon him, Saint George thrust with his lance, but it shattered into a thousand pieces as it made contact. He managed to remount, but the dragon swung its enormous tail and knocked him off his horse. The brave Knight was faint and dizzy from the fire of the monster's breath but he staggered to his feet and made the Sign of the Cross. His strength returned and he drew his sword Ascalon. In attempting another attack, the dragon exposed the softer part of its body beneath the wing, and it was there that Saint George thrust so deep that the dragon stood still, trembling.

Saint George knelt and offered a prayer of thanksgiving and then said to Princess Sabra, 'Undo the sash that is at your waist and tie it around the dragon's neck. You will not come to any harm'. With understandable trepidation she did as she was told and then he said, 'Now lead it to the market place in the city,' and, to her amazement, the dragon followed her meekly, like a lamb. When they arrived in the city, the people were ready to take to their heels, but Saint George told them not to be frightened of the dragon because it would terrorize them no more. With one blow of his sword Ascalon he put it to death and said, 'I do this to show the power of the good God, and to convert you to the one, true Faith'.

When the population realized that it was a Christian Knight who had overcome the dragon and made it meek as a lamb, they relinquished their false gods and became Christians. Princess Sabra was the first to be baptized, and it was not long before she was married to her true Knight, the brave Saint George of Merry England who had saved her from such a terrible death. Her father the King wanted to give Saint George half his kingdom, but the Saint asked him simply to take good care of God's churches, to honour the clergy, and have pity on the poor.

The Dragon in Saint John's Book of Revelation

In art, Saint George is frequently presented on horseback and tilting at the dragon that squirms below. The emblematic figure demonstrates that by faith and fortitude he conquered the Devil to whom Saint John refers as the Dragon in the Book of Revelation. "Now a great sign appeared in heaven; a woman adorned with the sun, standing on the moon and with the twelve stars on her head for a crown. She was pregnant, and in labour, crying aloud in the pangs of childbirth. Then a second sign appeared in the sky, a huge red dragon which had seven heads and ten horns, and each of the seven heads crowned with a coronet. Its tail dragged a third of the stars from the sky and dropped them to the earth, and the dragon stopped in front of the woman as she was having the child, so that he could eat it as soon as it was born from its mother. The woman brought a male child into the world, the son who was to rule all the nations with an iron sceptre, and the child was taken straight up to God and to his throne, while the woman escaped into the desert where God had made a place of safety ready for her.

And now war broke out in heaven, when Michael and his angels attacked the dragon. The dragon fought back with his angels, but they were defeated and driven out of heaven. The great dragon, the primeval serpent, known as the Devil or Satan, who had deceived all the world, was hurled down to the earth and his angels were hurled down with him ...The Serpent vomited water from his mouth like a river, after the woman to sweep her away in the current, but the earth came to her rescue; it opened its mouth and swallowed the river thrown up by the dragon's jaws" (*Rev* 12: 1-17). It is not surprising that icons of Saint George in the company of Saint Michael the Archangel featured widely in the piety and prayer of Christians in the East who believed that icons gave churches their sacred character.

Chivalry

Feudalism

Saint George's appearance in the *'Golden Legend'* as the "personification of chivalry" has been mentioned earlier and it may be useful to review the genesis of what became an expectation of knightly behaviour that had pious and religious dimensions.

During the years when the power of the Roman Empire was assailed by Barbarian invasions, small landowners at a distance from the capital felt particularly vulnerable to attack. If they lived near the estates of influential Roman patricians it seemed prudent to offer them their small parcels of land in exchange for protection. In time, these great Roman landowners numbered among their dependents many who cared little for personal responsibility and freedom, and were happy to serve their lord and master in any capacity as long as he clothed, fed, and protected them. From this evolved the custom of holding land in exchange for services, and men who tilled the soil throughout Europe, became the soldier-servants of a great lord or, in some cases, an abbot. They were free to make what income they could from their own agriculture, but had to work without wages on the lord's land and march under his banner when he decided to go to battle. Things changed when, instead of military service, a man could pay the lord a sum of money to hire better fighting men who were always ready to bear arms. Before long, covetous and acquisitive potentates fought one another, brought war to an area or, dissatisfied with a ruler, marched on a capital and plunged a nation into conflict.

The pages of history record such wars that may have been petty in theory but they inflicted dreadful suffering on peaceful folk, and brutalized European civilization by treading culture, religion and science underfoot. Fortunately, the Church inspired a spirit now remembered as chivalry that brought relief to troubled society. The knights of the Middle Ages who owned land that other men worked were able to ride their horses (Fr *'cheval'*, 'horse') throughout the world, searching for adventure and hearing from minstrels about the heroic deeds in the past that they could emulate. Most of all, they learned from the Church that to relieve those in distress was a worthy act and that respect for women was the mark of a noble spirit.

Geoffrey Chaucer presents the ideal knight in his *'Prologue to the Canterbury Tales'* as his pilgrims make their way to the tomb of Saint Thomas Becket. "There was a knight, a worthy man who loved chivalry, truth, honour, liberty, and 'courtesie'. No one had ridden farther than he in his lord's wars both in Christendom and in pagan countries, and everywhere he was honoured for his sterling qualities. He had fought for the Faith in Algeria …always had a reputation for honour and wisdom, and he conducted himself as modestly as a maiden. He had never said an unkind word to anyone in his life, and was a true, perfect, and gentle knight."

Amour Courtois, Courtly Love

Amour Courtois originated in the castle life of Aquitaine, Provence, Champagne and Burgundy around the time of the First Crusade, 1096-1099, and there are reports that a tribunal called the 'Court of Love' existed in Provence and Languedoc in which lords and ladies debated and decided questions of gallantry. It caught the imagination of the troubadour poets like Duke William of Aquitaine, 1071-1126 who, through their involvement in the enterprise, noticed that attitudes similar to courtly love were already expressed in Islamic writing. They adopted the terms of feudalism in declaring themselves the vassal of the lady who was the powerful head of the castle's household and culture, especially when the lord was away fighting for Christendom. Eleanor of Aquitaine brought the ideal of love based on character and action first to the court of France and then to England when she became

Henry II's Queen during the Chancellorship and Archbishopric of Saint Thomas Becket of Canterbury. Courtly love's appreciation of womanhood, as an ennobling spiritual and moral force, contributed to the reverence accorded to its peerless example, the Blessed Virgin Mary, and to the expansion of her shrines and pilgrimages. It was, for example, a Crusading knight Sir Geoffrey de Faverches who assigned lands and money for the maintenance of her shrine at Walsingham, and the establishment of a religious order to cherish it.

The literary convention 'Amour Courtois' throws light on the mediaeval chivalrous deeds of which Saint George and the Dragon is one. Gaston Paris first used the term in his 1883 article *'Sir Lancelot of the Round Table'* that was based upon the twelfth century work of Chretien de Troyes. It was a love ideally characterized by an idolizing and ennobling discipline in which a knight made himself worthy of a beautiful lady by behaving bravely and honourably. The expression became widely accepted and, in 1936, C.S. Lewis wrote his influential *'Allegory of Love'* identifying qualities of Courtly Love that included Humility, Courtesy and a love more akin to the Christian perception of *'Caritas'* (charity), though some scholars have preferred to detect a frustrated relationship of a physical nature, or reject the term as a modern invention because it appears only in a twelfth century Provencal poem as *'cortez amour'*. Others, however, appreciate it for its association with 'fin amour' (fine, pure love), that occurs frequently in French and German literature, and the many mediaeval stories describing a perception of a love that has courtliness at its essence. The thirteenth century allegorical love poem *'Romance of the Rose'* by Guillaume de Lorris satirized *'amour courtois'* with its elements of disappointment and sorrow, and the society that cultivated its unrealistic conventions.

The Round Table

The *'Sir Lancelot of the Round Table'* of Chretien de Troyes and Gaston Paris, calls to mind Saint George's sword 'Ascalon' and 'Excalibur', the similarly mystical sword of King Arthur who founded the Knights of the Round Table. King Cameliard, the father of Guinevere, Arthur's wife, sent him a round table so large that a hundred and fifty worthy knights could sit without anyone taking precedence. No higher dignity could be bestowed, and all were committed to honour, reverence for women, piety, and the relief of the oppressed. The wandering minstrels told the stories of their chivalry to the inspiration of later writers like Sir Thomas Mallory whose *'Morte d'Arthur'* summarized the legends of King Arthur, his reign, and the ultimate dissolution of the Round Table resulting from greed, treachery, and impious behaviour contrary to chivalry.

Unfortunately, in an imperfect world, not all the knights were like Galahad and Bedivere. In the nineteenth century *'Idylls of the King'* by Alfred Tennyson, the dying Arthur mourns the passing of chivalry:

> "Such a sleep they sleep – the men I loved – I think that we
> Shall never more, at any future time,
> Delight our souls with tales of knightly deeds..."

But he also holds out hope in a sublime perception of prayer as man's communication with his Creator:

> "Pray for my soul.
> More things are wrought by prayer
> Than this world dreams of.
> Wherefore let thy voice
> Rise like a fountain for me night and day
> For what are men better than sheep or goats
> That nourish a blind life within the brain,
> If, knowing God, they lift not hands of prayer
> Both for themselves and those who call them friend?
> For so the whole round earth is every way
> Bound by gold chains about the feet of God."

The chivalric concept of knighthood associated with an unselfish, chaste and obedient piety played some part in the establishment of monastic military orders like the Knights Templars who were founded in the twelfth century. They were also known as "The Poor Knights of Christ and of the Temple of Solomon," and the development of their rule has been ascribed to St Bernard of Clairvaux. For more than a hundred years they had a presence in the Holy Land, fought bravely in the Crusades, undertook a building programme, and were renowned protectors of pilgrims. Similarly, the Knights of Malta known as "The Military Hospitaler Order of St John of Jerusalem, of Rhodes and of Malta," have a long history of hospice work and military efforts on behalf of pilgrims.

Saint George, Patron and Titular Guardian

Patron of England and Soldiers

Saint George's patronage of England is related to pride in nationhood, and his care of soldiers and their military prowess that is attributable in part to the early reliance Byzantine armies placed on his help. The compelling reason why he is more officially the Patron of England, soldiers and associated professions is based on a report by William of Malmesbury. During the First Crusade, the Christian forces were led by Godfrey de Bouillon. Just before the Battle of Antioch in 1098, Saint George appeared to the Crusaders accompanied by Saint Demetrius of Sirmium, a fellow soldier who was martyred under Maximian early in the fourth century. "The martyr Knights" inspired a victory that increased Saint George's fame throughout Europe and the East, and encouraged soldiers to seek his protection and intercession. Devotion in England was focused and intensified during the Third Crusade, 1189-1192, led by Richard I, the 'Lion Heart' who placed his army under the protection of the Saint who appeared during an ultimately successful expedition against the Saracens.

The English flag

It was during Richard's reign that the "arms of Saint George" ("Argent, a cross, gules") was introduced, and his Red Cross on a white background became the English flag. As early as 1284, the emblem of a ship flying a white flag with a red cross adorned the official seal of Lyme Regis and other maritime towns, and a white flag with the red Cross of Saint George in the upper corner is still the White Ensign of the Royal Navy. By the fourteenth century, "Saint George's Arms" had become a feature of uniform for English soldiers and sailors. In the wardrobe accounts at the time of the battle of Crecy in 1346, a charge is made for "86 pennoncells (narrow, triangular, or swallow-tailed flags, or long, pointed streamers) of the arms of Saint George for the King's ship and 800 others for the men at arms." The arms were so reverenced that later, in the ordinances of Richard II, there is an instruction to every soldier in the English army that was invading Scotland to bear "a sign of the arms of Saint George both before and behind," while the pain of death is threatened against any of the enemy's soldiers "who do bear the same crosse or token of Saint George, even if they be prisoners."

At the beginning of the eighteenth century, the crowns of England and Scotland were united, and the white cross on a blue background of the Apostle Saint Andrew was added to that of Saint George. In 1801, when Ireland was united to England and Scotland, Saint Patrick's red cross on a white background was added to the Union Flag that was ingeniously arranged to give each cross equal prominence. The resultant Union Jack was not designed as a boastful standard of war, but to stand in memory of three brave and holy men who teach to love freedom, justice, peace, chivalry, and the love of God and His Blessed Mother, and of liberty, justice peace, and chivalry.

Saint Paul who preached Christ crucified says that the Cross was a sign of shame and disgrace, an instrument of execution that scandalized the pagans. Yet we can boast of Our Lord's Cross that presents God's saving power, and through which He effects reconciliation with all humanity. In the New Testament, the Cross symbolizes the act of Redemption, and the imitation of Christ who asks His followers to take up their daily cross and walk in His footsteps. The practice of signing oneself with the Cross is mentioned by Tertullian in the second century, and the associated Feasts are the Exaltation of the Cross on September 14th, and the Finding of the Cross by Saint Helena, the mother of the emperor Constantine, on May 3rd until 1960 (cf. *Gal* 5:11, 6:14; *Ph* 2:8, *Heb* 12:2, *1 Co* 1:17-18, 23, 2:2, *Mt* 10:38; *Mk* 8:34; *Lk* 9:23, 14:27).

As early as 1222, Saint George's Day was decreed by the national synod of Oxford to be kept as a lesser feast on April 23rd. In 1415, after the Battle of Agincourt when Henry V famously invoked him as England's Patron, the Archbishop of Canterbury, Cardinal Henry Chichele elevated Saint George's Day to one of the principal feasts in the Liturgical Calendar. Later, King Edward III, 1327-1377 and his warrior son, the Black (armoured) Prince of Wales, commended their military campaigns to the care of Saint George and "advanced banners" in his name. In the seventeenth and eighteenth centuries it was a Holy Day of Obligation in England, but after 1778 it became a simple devotion though ranked as a Double of the First Class with an Octave. The Revised Roman Calendar of 1969 made it an Optional Memorial for the Universal Church, but it remains a Feast in England and Wales.

Saint George has also been adopted at various times by Portugal, Aragon, the Republic of Genoa, Venice with Saint Mark, Russia, Ethiopia, and Catalonia, all seeing him as the example of chivalry *par excellence*. During the fourteenth century, Germany, Hungary and Sweden included him among the "Fourteen Holy Helpers". The list sometimes varied but the other thirteen were usually Saints Acacius, Barbara, Blaise, Catherine of Alexandria, Denys, Erasmus, Eustace, Giles, Margaret of Antioch, Pantaleon, Christopher and Vitus. Most were venerated as martyrs and the intercession of all was sought in a variety of demanding or hazardous situations, for the cure of certain illnesses, the warding off of evil spirits, and for a peaceful death. Motorists, golfers threatened by lightning, sore throat and epilepsy sufferers will, for example, recognize the respective involvement of Saints Christopher, Barbara, and Vitus. Saint George himself was invoked against the plague and leprosy. Six English Kings have been baptized with the Saint's name and in addition to the significantly important churches in Palestine, Rome, Constantinople, Venice and Verona, one hundred and sixty have been dedicated to him in England over the centuries. In Westminster Cathedral, the Mother Church of Catholics in England there is a chapel of Saint George and the English Martyrs, and the Cathedral of the Southwark Archdiocese bears his name.

The Feast of Saint George

Prayers

Lord, you have given us cause to rejoice in the merits and intercession of your blessed martyr George. Grant that we who seek your favours through him may obtain them as a gift of your grace (*Collect of the Liturgy of the Feast*).

Lord, hear the prayers of those who praise your mighty power. As Saint George was ready to follow Christ in suffering and death, so may he be ready to help us in our weakness (*Opening Prayer of the Liturgy*).

Lord, bless our offerings and make them holy. May these gifts fill our hearts with the love which gave Saint George victory over all his suffering (*Offertory Prayer over the Gifts*).

Lord, we receive your gifts from heaven on this joyful feast. May we who proclaim at this holy Table the death and resurrection of your Son, come to share His glory with Saint George and all your holy Martyrs (*Prayer after Communion*).

Scripture

The One sitting on the throne spoke, 'Now I am making the whole of creation new,' He said. 'Write this: that what I am saying is sure and will come true.' And then He said, 'It is already done. I am the Alpha and Omega, the Beginning and the End. I will give water from the well of life free to anybody who is thirsty; it is the rightful inheritance of the one who proves victorious; and I will be his God and he a son to me (*Rev* 21:5-7).

To all Jesus said, 'If anyone wants to be a follower of mine, let him renounce himself and take up his cross every day and follow me. For anyone who wants to save his life will lose it, but anyone who loses his life for my sake, that man will save it. What gain then, is it for a man to have won the whole world and to have lost or ruined his very self? For if anyone is ashamed of me and of my words, of him the Son of Man will be ashamed when He comes in His own glory an in the glory of the Father and the holy angels. (*Luke* 9:23-26)

By St Peter Damian

Saint George was transported from one kind of military service to another, since he laid aside the earthly office of tribune to join the ranks of the army of Christ. Like a truly keen soldier, he threw away the burden of his earthly possessions by giving all he had to the poor, thus free and unencumbered and wearing the breastplate of faith, he advanced into the thick of the fray, a valiant soldier of Christ. From this we learn a clear lesson, that nobody can fight properly and boldly for the faith if he clings to a fear of being stripped of earthly possessions.

Saint George, aflame with the fire of the Holy Spirit and invincibly defended by the banner of the Cross, not only fought with a wicked king but defeated also the Prince of all the wicked in the person of his minion, and encouraged the soldiers of Christ to bear themselves valiantly. Clearly, he had at his side the supreme and invisible judge, who by his free choice allowed the hands of the wicked to wreak their violence even on Saint George. Although God gave the body of His martyr over to murderers, he guarded his soul with unceasing protection, defended as it was by the unconquerable fortress of faith.

Let us not merely admire this soldier of the heavenly army: let us also imitate him. Let us raise up our spirits to think on that heavenly reward, and fix our hearts on it in contemplation, and so never flinch whether the world smiles on us with its blandishments or menaces us with adversities. Let us purify ourselves, according to Saint Paul's advice, from every uncleanness of body and soul, so that we too may in time be worthy to enter that temple of blessedness on which our minds are fixed.

Whoever wishes to sacrifice himself to God in the tabernacle of Christ, which is the Church, must first be made clean by washing in the sacred font, and then be clothed in various garments, that is, virtues, as it is written: 'Your priests shall be clothed in justice.' For he who in Baptism is reborn as a new man in Christ, must not put on the signs of his mortality; he must put away the old man and put on the new and live in Him, being made new himself by striving to live a pure life. And so, purged of the stain of our old sin and shining with the brightness of our new way of life, we can worthily celebrate the paschal mystery and truly imitate the example of the blessed martyrs. (*Sermon of Saint Peter Damian, Office of Readings*, April 23rd).

Hymns to Saint George

Leader now on earth no longer,
Soldier of the Eternal King,
Victor in the fight for heaven,
we thy loving praises sing.
Praise him, who in deadly
battle never shrank from foeman's sword,
Proof against all earthly weapon,
gave his life for Christ Our Lord.

Who, when earthly war was over,
fought but not for earth's renown;
Fought and won a nobler glory
– won the martyr's purple crown.
Help us when temptation presses;
we have still our crown to win;
Help us when our soul is weary,
fighting with the powers of sin.
Clothe us in thy shining armour;
place thy good sword in our hand;
Teach us how to wield it,
fighting onwards towards the Heavenly Land.
Great Saint George, our Patron help us,
in our conflict be thou nigh;
Help us in that daily battle
where each one must win or die.
(*J.W. Reeks, 1849-1900*).

To George our Saint thou gavest grace
without one fear all foes to face,
And to confess by faithful death that
Word of Life which was his breath,
O keep us Helper of Saint George
to fear no bonds that man can forge.
Arm us like him who in Thy trust
beat down the dragon to the dust;

So that we too may tread down sin
and with Thy Saints a crown may win.
Help us, O God,
that we may be a land acceptable to Thee.
(*Laurence Houseman, 1865-1959*).

Jesus, Lord of Our Salvation,
for Thy warrior bold and true,
Now accept our thankful praises
and our strength do Thou renew,
That, like George, with courage dauntless
we may all our foes subdue.
Blazoned on our country's banner
England bears the knightly sign;
Lord, our fatherland empower that,
endued with strength divine,
She may evermore with courage bear
the standard that is Thine.
(*F.W. Newman 1856-1934*).

The poetry recalls again the importance of the Cross.
The mission of Our Lord's first coming is complete,
and the healing miracles He accomplished in His life,
death and Resurrection await the perfection of His
second coming and final victory over evil. The universe
is good because God, its Creator, is infinitely good, and

in His Son we are redeemed once and for all so, in the light of eternity, the struggle between good and evil is over. The world of time, however, remains beset by temptations, plagues, wars, inhumanity, suffering, and death, the present evils that God tolerates in the achievement of salvation.

In honouring her many soldier-martyrs, the Church tells us that sanctity is attainable in whatever state of life to which we are called, as we fulfil our Christian duties and turn the circumstances and events of life into occasions of serving God. Our Lord's true disciples are martyrs in their disposition of heart, their readiness to lose all and suffer anything rather than offend God. They are martyrs by way of the patience and courage with which they bear all trials and their readiness to take up their own cross and share in His Passion. In this life we suffer anxiety, disappointment, injustice, hardship, enmity, danger, and the pains of mind and body. Even our own faults and weaknesses are burdens to be borne patiently if we are to possess our souls in peace and charitably understand our neighbours' similar problems. Life then becomes the opportunity for heroic virtue in the spirit of Christian patience that is the martyrdom of all Christ's disciples.

The Orders of Saint George

The Most Noble Order of the Garter

Edward III founded this honoured company of twenty-five Knights and the Sovereign in 1348 "for the advancement of piety, nobility and chivalry", and it is the highest British civil and military honour. Later, a chapter of canons and impoverished knights chosen for valour and their needs were associated with them and shared their Chapel. It is thought that the King wanted to revive the qualities and initial motivation of the Round Table of Arthurian legend by creating such a gathering, and the Garter to be a symbol of the reverence and homage due to women. The story of this choice of symbol is that when he was dancing at a ball held in Calais with the celebrated beauty Joan of Kent, Countess of Salisbury and later the wife of the Black Prince, one of her blue stockings slipped to the floor. As onlookers sniggered, he picked it up, put it on his own knee, and admonished the courtiers with the words that remain the Order's motto, "Honi soit qui mal y pense", "Shame to anyone who thinks evil of this."

The King admirably envisaged the Order of the Garter as "a Society, Fellowship, College of Knights wherein all are equal, to represent how they ought to be united in all Chances and various Turns of Fortune; co-partners in Peace and War, assistant to one another in all serious and dangerous exploits: and though the whole course of their lives to show Fidelity and Friendliness one towards another." The blue garter was to signify "a lasting bond of Friendship and Honour." With some enlightened self-interest, Edward had also harnessed the idealism of chivalry to his own cause and had put the greatest names in the land under an honourable obligation of duty to himself.

The Order's insignia comprises the Garter emblazoned with the *"Honi soit..."* motto, a star with Saint George's Cross, and a jewel encrusted collar with a badge depicting the Saint slaying the Dragon, and was worn for the first time at a tournament at Eltham in 1348. The Chapel dedicated to "Saint George of Merry England" and designed as the Order's official sanctuary was developed by Edward IV and completed by Henry VII "in honour of Almighty God and His Mother Mary the Glorious Virgin, and Saint George the Martyr." It ranks next to Westminster Abbey as a royal mausoleum and it became customary for royal funerals to be conducted there. The Feast of Saint George on April 23rd is also the Feast of the Order.

In addition to suggestions of happiness, the frequently used description "merry" has connotations of relief, liberation, good order, a Christian "England's green and pleasant land" that is Mary's Dowry, the desire to preserve a golden age of chivalry and its noble deeds that continue to stir the imagination. There is resonance of humanity's cyclical nostalgia for the good old days that may not have been all that good, but fortunately inspires a quest for a brave new world and sunny uplands still to be attained. Shakespeare incomparably expresses the evocation:

> This royal throne of kings, this sceptred isle.
> This earth of majesty, this seat of mars,
> This other Eden, demi-Paradise;
> This fortress built by Nature for herself
> Against infection and the hand of war;
> This happy breed of men, this little world,
> This precious stone set in a silver sea,
> This blessed plot, this earth, this realm, this England,
> This nurse, this teeming womb of royal kings,
> Fear'd by their breed and famous by their birth,
> Renowned for their deeds as far from home,
> For Christian service and true chivalry,
> As is the sepulchre in stubborn Jewry
> Of the world's Ransom, blessed Mary's Son.
> (*King Richard II 2 i*)

On Saint George's Day, 1349, while London was still plagued by the Black Death, the first service of the Order of the Garter was conducted at Windsor, every knight in plumes and the garter-blue robes taking his place in the stalls. The King carried a great two-handed sword that still hangs behind the altar of Saint George's Chapel.

The Most Distinguished Order of Saint Michael and St George

This Order of Knights and Companions was founded in 1818 by the Prince regent, later King George IV. Once again, Saint George is associated with his eminent predecessor in the task of vanquishing Dragons (cf. *Rev* 12).

Knights in Honour of Saint George

In 1470, the Emperor Frederick IV instituted an order of Knights in honour of Saint George; and there is evidence that the Venetians also dedicated an honourable military order to him.

Saint George in Art, Drama, and Verse

Art

The earliest reference in art to the story of Saint George and the Dragon is on an old Roman tombstone that was found at Conisborough in Yorkshire. The Princess is shown to be already in the clutches of the dragon while an abbot looks on and blesses her rescuer.

During the Middle Ages in England, the development of art was centred largely on the Church, its inspiration, and its architecture. For example, the enthusiasm for carved ornamentation meant that, among the leaves and flowers of the woods and fields, stone masons frequently carved favourite figures like the Lamb of God and Saint George fighting the Dragon.

Examples of Saint George holding a white banner with a Red Cross are on the roodscreens at Hempstead and Filby in Norfolk. The Norman font at Thorpe Arnold in Leicestershire has an engraving of him, this time battling with two dragons.

'George and the Dragon' by Paolo Ucelli has a numinous quality that is appropriate for a depiction of the ongoing conflict between good and evil. *'Saint George'* by Andrea Mantegna, the Venice Academy. *'The Holy*

Family with Saint George' by Giovannt Bellini, the
Venice Academy. *'Saint George and the Dragon'* by
Vittore Carpaccio, the Hospital of St George of
Schiovani, Venice. *'Saint George'*, and *'Saint George and
the Dragon'* by Albert Durer. *'The Princess leads the
Dragon to the Market Place'* by Thomas Maybank. *'The
Quest of Saint George'* by Frank O. Salisbury. The statue
of Saint George carved by Donatello.

Drama

During the Middle Ages, dramatic presentations helped to
teach religious faith to the people, especially those who did
not have access to books, or were unable to read. They were
called *'Miracle Plays'* because they were generally about the
marvels worked by popular saints like Saint George whose
tussle with the Dragon even became the inspiration for many
an inn-sign. Comical interludes that gave light relief were
"merry-making" scenes and antics that are still replicated in
the pantomimes of today. Scholars refer to dramas inspired
by sacred Scripture as *'Mystery Plays'* to distinguish them
from the *'Miracles'*, because they dealt only with Gospel
events. The *'Moralities'* of the fifteenth century like,
'Everyman', that accompanied and followed the *'Miracles'*
with simple action and edifying purpose, were dramatic
verses in which the biblical characters and saints gave way
to personified abstractions of the 'Virtues and Vices'.

Verse

'Piers Plowman', the alliterative poem by William Langland, 1330-1400, includes narratives of the life of Our Lord in which His identity merges with that of the humble and exploited peasant who "maintained the state of the world, but was receiving less than justice." The poem's underlying theme is divine mercy, and the sacrifice of the Cross that asks for honest work and loving kindness. It voiced the recurring English reaction to the contrast between misused wealth and undeserved destitution, and a characteristic resolve not to destroy society but to redress the balance. At the end of the fourteenth and beginning of the fifteenth centuries, paintings by obviously devout but unskilled amateurs appeared on the walls of parish churches. In many, Our Lord, the "Christ of the Trades", appeared scourged and bleeding, and carrying His carpenter's tools of mallet, hammer, knife, axe and pincers. This figure was found in many churches as far apart as Suffolk and Pembrokeshire and, at Hessett in Suffolk, the labouring Christ faces a painting of Saint George, the hero of knightly chivalry overcoming the dragon.

The influence of the *'Moralities'* is seen in the *'Faerie Queen'* by Edmund Spenser, 1552-1599, in which twelve knights exemplifying different virtues undertake adventures with chivalrous and historical resonance. Arthur symbolizes 'Magnificence' in the Aristotelian

sense of the perfection of all virtues; the Red Cross
Knight protects Virginity in the person of the princess
Una, and slays the dragon that had imprisoned her royal
parents in a castle; Guyan is the knight of Temperance;
Belphoebe and Britomart stand for Chastity; Triamond
and Cambell demonstrate Friendship; Artegall is the
Knight of Justice; Calidore is the knight of Courtesy.
Most of all, in this allegory of Moral Virtue, Saint George
stands for Christianity. After the Red Cross Knight has
overcome the dragon, released the prisoners, and become
engaged to the princess, Spenser captures the reaction to
the epithet "merry" in the context of England's Patron.

> Great joy was made that day of young and old,
> And solemn feast proclaimed throughout the land
> That exceeding mirth may not be told;
> Suffice it here by sign to understand
> The usual joys of at knitting of love's band:
> Thrice happy man the Knight himself did hold
> Possessed of his lady's heart and hand ...
>
> Thou among those saints which thou dost see
> Shalt be a saint, and their own nation's friend
> And Patron: thou Saint George shall called be
> Saint George of merry England, the sign of victory.